A PROSE ANTHOLOGY
OF THE
FIRST WORLD WAR

Selected and edited by Robert Hull

See that little stream – we could walk to it in two
minutes. It took the British a month to walk to it
– a whole empire walking very slowly, dying in
front and pushing forward behind. And another
empire walked very slowly backward a few
inches a day, leaving the dead like a million
bloody rags. No European will ever do that
again in this generation.
F Scott Fitzgerald[1]

Wayland

Prose Anthologies of War

A Prose Anthology of the First World War

A Prose Anthology of the Second World War

First published in 1992 by
Wayland (Publishers) Ltd
61 Western Road, Hove
East Sussex BN3 1JD

© Copyright 1992 Wayland (Publishers) Ltd

Editor: Catherine Ellis
Designer: David Armitage
Picture editor: Shelley Noronha
Consultant: John Rowley, history advisory teacher at the South-West Divisional Professional
    Centre, Southampton

British Cataloguing in Publication Data
Prose Anthology of the First World War
    I. Hull, Robert
    940.3

ISBN 0 7502 0452 4

Typeset by Dorchester Typesetting Group Limited
Printed and bound by Butler and Tanner Ltd, Frome and London

Acknowledgements
For permission to reproduce illustrations the publishers gratefully acknowledge the Imperial
War Museum, which supplied all photographs except the following: Mary Evans 8; Billie Love
48; Topham pp. 3, 16, 21, 53; Peter Newark's Western Americana p. 24, 35; Wayland Picture
Library p. 45.

For permission to use copyright text the publishers gratefully acknowledge the following:
Alan Sutton Publishing for John Laffin's *British Butchers and Bunglers of World War I*; George
Allen & Unwin for J W Graham's *Conscription and Conscience*; Bodley Head for F Scott Fitzgerald's *Tender is the Night*; Buchverlage Ullstein Langen Müller for Manfred von Richthofen's
The Red Barron; Carcanet Press Ltd and Myfanwy Thomas for *Under Storm's Wing* by Helen
Thomas; Constable Publishers for M Aldrich's *A Hill Top on the Marne*; Paolo Monelli's *Toes Up*
by permission of Duckworth; Paul Fussell's *The Great War and Modern Memory*, by permission
of Oxford University Press; A J P Taylor's *The First World War: An Illustrated History*, reproduced by permission of Penguin Books Ltd, and G P Putnam; extracts from *Voices and Images of
the Great War*, *The Roses of No Man's Land* and *1914* all by Lyn Macdonald reproduced by permission of Penguin Books Ltd; extracts from Chapman's *Vain Glory* reprinted by permission of
the Peters Fraser & Dunlop Group Ltd; Sidgwick & Jackson for Malcolm Brown's *IWM Book of
The First World War* and William Pressey's *All For A Shilling A Day*; H F & G Witherby Ltd for
Flora Sandes's *Autobiography of a Woman Soldier*. While every attempt has been made to trace
copyright holders, in some cases it has proved impossible. The publishers apologise for this
apparent negligence.

Contents

Introduction

In the last extract in this book, Paul Fussell describes how he walked over one of the battlefields of the First World War, more than fifty years after it had ended, and could smell 'rusted iron everywhere'. It was as if the land itself could not forget. In the same way, the public memory of the Great War, as it is often called, still surrounds us near our own homes, in thousands of monuments in the many countries that sent troops to the fighting. In town parks, on village squares, in city centres on every continent, you see commemorative statues and read lists, engraved in stone, of those who died.

We remember it in other ways. The 1914-18 war was recorded in innumerable photographs, many of them shocking or disturbing. It was filmed, and reported on by journalists, in newspapers that people could buy next day just behind the trenches. It was re-created in images of desolation by artists like the English painter Paul Nash.

It is remembered in individual stories too. Millions of words survive from those years, in letters, diaries and memoirs written by soldiers, nurses, chaplains and others at the front – often against army regulations – and by the families and loved ones who waited at home. We can read in them the innermost thoughts of people who lived through those appalling times. We can almost imagine how it was for the family of Trooper Mason, who didn't want him to enlist, and for the Romanian Octavian Taslaunan, who had to fight to help preserve someone else's empire.

In the years leading up to 1914, there were six huge European empires, each of them edgy about the others, and increasingly determined not to let a scrap of advantage go to the other nations. When Austria declared war on Serbia in July 1914 it was inevitable that it would soon become a world war: Germany, Turkey and Austria-Hungary were on one side; Britain, Russia and France on the other, helped by the Dutch, the Belgians and the Italians (the Allies).

The battle of empires soon spread, like cracks in breaking ice, all across Europe, and beyond. There was fighting in Africa and the Middle East, and there were even two naval battles in the South Atlantic. In 1917 the USA joined the Allies.

An enormous war. The first war to involve such enormous numbers of people, both civilians and military, or cause such death and mutilation – twenty million dead and wounded. The first war in history, perhaps, in which ordinary civilians came under such deliberate, terrorizing attack. At the end of it, three of the empires – German, Turkish and Austro-Hungarian – were broken up by the Treaty of Versailles.

Such huge events as the First World War are mass movements, the landslides of history. But these landslides are made up of millions of tiny slipping grains of individual experience. Fortunately for us when we want to understand it, in the First World War many of these experiences were written down and collected.

The individual memories, the grains of history gathered in this book, say something truthful about a war that happened only eighty years ago. They are a bit of history, the history that reminds you where you come from. And if you don't know where you come from, how do you know who you are?

TO WAR

After years of rivalry and changing alliances, the outbreak of war came suddenly, sparked off by the assassination of Austrian Archduke Franz Ferdinand in Bosnia on 28 June 1914. The war was to involve huge empires; countries all round the world sent soldiers to the battlefields. Here is how the summons came to a Russian Cossack village on the border of Mongolia. Stephen Graham, who was a well-known British travel writer, was in the village at the time.

At 4 a.m. on 31 July the first telegram came through; an order to mobilize and be prepared for active service. I was awakened that morning by an unusual commotion, and, going into the village street, saw the soldier population collected in groups, talking excitedly. My peasant hostess cried out to me, 'Have you heard the news? There is war.' A young man on a fine horse came galloping down the street, a great red flag hanging from his shoulders and flapping in the wind, and as he went he called out the news to each and every one, 'War! War!'

. . . .

Then a rumour went round, 'It is with England, with England.' So far away these people lived they did not know that our old hostility had vanished. Only after four days did something like the truth come to us, and then nobody believed it.

'An immense war,' said a peasant to me. 'Thirteen powers engaged – England, France, Russia, Belgium, Bulgaria, Serbia, Montenegro, Albania, against Germany, Austria, Italy, Romania, Turkey.'

Two days after the first telegram a second came, and this one called up every man between the ages of eighteen and forty-three. Astonishing that Russia should at the very outset begin to mobilize its reservists 5,000 *versts* from the scene of hostilities!

. . . .

On Thursday, the day of setting out, there came a third telegram from St Petersburg. The vodka shop, which had been locked and sealed during the great temperance struggle which had been in progress in Russia, might be opened for one day only – the day of mobilization. After that day, however, it was to be closed again and remain closed until further orders.

What scenes there were that day![2]

Verst   *A Russian measure of length, about 1 km.*
Temperance   *Abstinence from alcohol.*

Ernst Fischer, who became a soldier in the Austrian Army, watched the mad fervour in the streets of Graz after war was declared. Angry at the Serbian assassination of Archduke Franz Ferdinand, some Austrians began to attack anyone they thought was a Serb.

Awkward young soldiers were being pelted with flowers by women and girls. The streets of Graz were full of excited people marching towards the Sudbahnhof. Their patriotism reeked of alcohol. Over and over came the roar: 'Death to all Serbs! Long live the Emperor! Down with traitors!' Outside the station, in the middle of a row of insane, screaming people, a man was dragged to the ground, trampled on, torn limb from limb. 'A Serbian spy!' someone called out. 'A Serbian spy!' went the cry from one mouth to another as the remains of a human being were retrieved from the murderous mob.[3]

Sudbahnhof   South railway station.

On 1 August, Germany declared war on Russia, and two days later on France. The day after that, the 4th, Germany and Britain were at war. The *Daily Mail* newspaper, in London, had tips about how to express the new hatreds.

Readers should refuse service from a German or Austrian waiter.

Though he was a Romanian, Octavian Taslaunan lived in Sibiiu, a town just over the Romanian border in Hungary. He was called up to join the Austro-Hungarian Army, and as his train carried him towards the war he mused on the 'ignominy', or dishonour, of fighting for a foreign country.

The ignominy of going out to fight, and perhaps die, God knows where, as a Hungarian soldier made me tremble with indignation. I saw myself dead, with the Hungarian colours on my breast, and I heard myself carried to the grave to the sound of the Szoszad instead of our 'Rest in Peace.' . . . What a horrible farce!

Each wayside station resounded with the weeping and wailing of women. I gave up leaning out of the window, as the spectacle of so much misery was too much for me. And yet, after a time, this universal sorrow restored a sense of calm. War is like a cataclysm. It makes no selection of its victims. Why should I not bear the blows of fate as well as any other man? . . . Besides, our numbers grew at every halt.

However, it was not for nothing that I found myself among all these Romanians. I still entertained a hope.

There was not the slightest sign of enthusiasm anywhere. We might have been a company of the dead until we reached Fàgàras. Like slaves we responded to the summons of our master, even a summons to our death. But at the bottom of our hearts there lurked the hope of a terrible vengeance.[4]

Szoszad   A traditional Hungarian song.
Fàgàras   A small town in Romania.

The families of enlisting soldiers were often not very happy. British Trooper F Mason's was one of those who were less enthusiastic.

I never said anything about enlisting when I went home that night and on the Sunday morning there was an OHMS envelope. I didn't open it. So when breakfast started Mother said, 'What's that? Get it opened.' I didn't want to open it but she insisted. The instructions were to report to the Drill Hall, Grange Road, Middlesborough. When I read that out, 'Jack,' she said to Dad, 'stop his gallop. He doesn't go! There's lots that will go before that boy goes.' So Dad said, 'Have you joined, Pete?' I said, 'Yes, Dad.' 'Well,' he said, 'this is a nice how-do-you-do.'

Then Mother started to get excited. She said, 'Stop his gallop, Dad. You see Chief Constable Riches. He's not going.' So Dad said, 'Well, just supposing, Pete, you came back with a leg or an arm off? Who wants you?' I said, 'Let me get there first, Dad, before I get back.' 'So,' he said, 'It's alright you talking like that but you don't know what you've done.' I said, 'But I do know what I've done.' 'Alright,' he said, 'if you've made your bed, you'll have to lie in it.' I said, 'I'll lie in it, Dad.' 'Well,' he said to Mother, 'there's no more to be said, Polly.' And that was the start.[5]

OHMS   *On His Majesty's Service*

THE BEGINNING –
ORDINARY PEOPLE

On 3 August 1914, Germany invaded Belgium and Luxembourg, and then moved quickly on into France. Civilians all over Europe were caught up in the fighting that was now beginning. Mildred Aldrich, an American living in France, watched war come to her 'beloved panorama'.

A dozen times during the afternoon I went into the study and tried to read. Little groups of old men, women, and children were in the road, mounted on the barricade which the English had left. I could hear the murmur of their voices. In vain I tried to stay indoors. The thing was stronger than I, and in spite of myself, I would go out on the lawn and, field-glass in hand, watch the smoke. To my imagination every shot meant awful slaughter, and between me and the terrible thing stretched a beautiful country, as calm in the sunshine as if horrors were not. In the field below me the wheat was being cut. I remembered vividly afterward that a white horse was drawing the reaper, and women and children were stacking and gleaning. Now and then the horse would stop, and a woman, with her red handkerchief on her head, would stand, shading her eyes a moment, and look off. Then the white horse would turn and go plodding on. The grain had to be got in if the Germans were coming, and these fields were to be trampled as they were in 1870.

It was just about six o'clock when the first bomb that we could really see came over the hill. The sun was setting. For two hours we saw them rise, descend, explode. Then a little smoke would rise from one hamlet, then from another; then a tiny flame – hardly more than a spark – would be visible; and by dark the whole plain was on fire,

lighting up Mareuil in the foreground, silent and untouched. There were long lines of grain-stacks and mills stretching along the plain. One by one they took fire, until, by ten o'clock, they stood like a procession of huge torches across my beloved panorama.[6]

Mareuil   *A town in France.*

As the German armies crossed into the neutral country of Belgium in August 1914, many people abandoned their homes and fled. Ernst Toller, a German soldier, wandered round an empty village.

Here the people had only left their homes because the war had driven them away; they could take no more with them than they could carry in their arms, and every room told of some painful choice. In one a woman had bundled all her bed-linen together, and then left it lying. In another a dress had been torn from the wardrobe only to be finally discarded. In another the mother or the child had collected a heap of toys and tied them up, only to abandon them at the last minute.

In the silence of this forsaken village there was nobody to question me, as I said out loud, as if one of those poor people had stood there:

'This had to be.'

I hurried away. There was no one in sight; from whom was I escaping?[7]

Of one town in northern France, which looked completely deserted but wasn't quite, Madame Deron recorded in her diary at the time.

The town is deserted, all the shops are shut up and the people have sealed themselves into their houses, joining up with neighbours for company. Bapaume is almost empty and the men who are left have hidden themselves for fear of capture. Our butcher spends the whole day concealed in a tree! Others shut themselves in cupboards or even in grandfather clocks.[8]

Soon there were thousands of people on the roads, forced out of their homes by the German advance. As Isabelle Rimbaud, sister of the famous French poet, Arthur Rimbaud, was preparing to leave her home near the Belgian border, she saw refugees passing her house. For some reason, many were dressed in their Sunday best clothes.

Saturday, 29 August 1914

While I am making the last preparations for departure, outside, in the burning heat, I see a confused rushing to and fro of military material, amid which the tragic film of emigration unrolls itself without ceasing: people on foot, wagons and carts piled with heterogeneous articles on which are huddled old men and sick, sheltered by an awning stretched over poles made fast in the four corners of the vehicle. Cows, colts, calves are driven as best may be through the general confusion. The men are gloomy, all of them. Many of them have put on their best clothes, probably thinking that thus they will score off the enemy, and one has the sad and ridiculous spectacle of provincial and countrified women hobbling along on Louis XV heels, much damaged by walking, suffocating in small corsets and tight-fitting, rumpled, dirty skirts, wearing over their dejected faces hats trimmed with showy plumes, and displaying sunburnt throats through the scallop of their low-cut blouses.[9]

Stephen Graham, the travel writer, saw similar scenes of displaced people on the other side of Europe, in Poland.

In many of the villages in Poland the people have buried their boots and spare clothes, with their money, and you are astonished to see the Polish peasants going about with bare feet or in straw slippers. They say that the German soldiers come and pull the boots off their feet to put into their forage sacks. Alas! the Germans are as keen as terriers at finding things that have been buried, and the peasants when they return to villages forsaken a week before, find that their things have all been dug up and taken away.[10]

In Russia Stephen Graham heard several stories of children who ran away from home to the war, either to help nurse the wounded or even to join in the fighting.

One of the phenomena which show how popular the war is in Russia is the participation of the children in the conflict. There is scarcely a town school in Russia from which boys have not run away to the war. Hundreds of girls have gone off in boys' clothes and tried to pass themselves off as boys and enlist as volunteers, and several have got through, since the medical examination is only a negligible formality required in one place, forgotten in another; the Russians

are so fit as a whole. So among the wounded in the battle of the Nieman was a broad-shouldered, vigorous girl from Zlato-Ust, only sixteen years old, and nobody had dreamed that she was other than the man for whom she was passing herself off. But not only boys and girls of sixteen and seventeen, but children of eleven and twelve have contrived to have a hand either in the fighting or in the nursing.

Whilst I was in Vilna there was a touching case – a little girl of twelve years, Marusia Charushina, turned up. She had run away from her home in Viatka, some thousand miles away, had got on the train as a 'hare,' i.e. without a ticket. The conductor had smiled on her and let her go on. At Vilna, in the traffic of the great Polish city, she was a little bewildered, but she asked a passing soldier the way to a hospital; he took her to one, and she explained to him that she had come to nurse the wounded. At the hospital a Red Cross nurse questioned her, and she gave the same answer. The nurse telegraphed to the little girl's father, and asked his permission that she should remain in the hospital nursing the wounded soldiers. The father gave permission, so little Marusia was allowed to remain. A uniform was made for her, and now as the smallest Sister of Mercy among them all she tends the soldiers and is very popular.[11]

SOLDIERS

If the refugees were bewildered by the war, many soldiers also found what was happening hard to believe. A British army officer, Lieutenant K B Tower, does what he's trained to do, but finds it strange.

23 August

I was out visiting my sentries in the woods about a thousand yards in advance of our position about 7 a.m. and was talking to an old Reservist, when we suddenly saw a horseman ride through the wood. He dismounted and tied his horse to a tree and advanced (about 300 yards from us) to the edge of the wood and stood looking at our position on the canal bank. My old Reservist said to me, 'Is that a German, Sir?' I said, 'Yes, I expect it is.' Whereupon he said, 'Shall I shoot him, Sir?' And I said, 'Yes, have a try.'

He picked up his rifle, took careful aim and fired. The man fell, and we walked over to look at him. He was a trooper of the famous Regiment of the Death's Head Hussars – the first German I had seen.

So I took his horse and rode it back to our lines and made my report. I then returned to the sentries in front and before I got there I heard heavy rifle fire from our detachment on the main road. The next moment I saw a German officer with a heavy limp come running in my direction. I ran after him, and he held up his hands and shouted in English, 'I am Count von Arnim'. He was slightly wounded in the leg and was shivering with fright. It appeared he was one of an officers' Cavalry patrol who had ridden down the road and had been caught by the fire of our post on the road. They were all hit.

By this time the sun was getting quite hot. A gorgeous morning. The church bells were ringing and the Belgian peasants could be seen walking quietly to church. What a contrast! It seemed hardly believable that we were at war and that men had just been killed only a few yards away. I was just returning to my sentries when a terrific fire opened on us from the woods to the north and my sentries came running in.[12]

This naïvety and lack of experience could have terrible consequences. William Pressey, a British gunner in the Royal Artillery, suddenly realized, looking back at a troop of French cavalry that had ridden past, that they had no idea of what they were attacking.

Coming towards us were a troop of French cavalry. I should say a hundred and fifty or two hundred strong. Gosh, but they looked splendid. I think word must have got to them about the German cavalry harassing us and they had come to put a stop to that. They could never have been told about the machine guns. They laughed and waved their lances at us, shouting 'Le Bosch fini'. What a picture they made with sunlight gleaming on their lances. We slowed down as they trotted briskly past, and everyone was looking back at them.

Before reaching the top of the hill they opened out to about six feet between each horse and in a straight line. We hardly breathed. Over the top of the hill they charged, lances at the ready.

There was not a sound from us. Then, only a few seconds after they disappeared, the hellish noise of machine guns broke out. We just looked at each other. The only words I heard spoken were 'Bloody hell . . .'. That's what it must have been over that hill, for not one man came back. Several of their horses did, and trotted beside us, and were collected at our next stopping place.

If only the cavalry officer had stopped for one minute and talked to our officers they would have told them of the mounted machine guns, and that it was certain death over the hill from where we had come. Who had sent that splendid troop to certain death? Surely all the conditions should have been known before sending lances against machine guns. If they were known, did anyone think the Germans would leave their machine guns and fight evenly, lance to lance? What an awful waste of husbands, brothers, sons. Many commanders of the war must have a lot on their minds.[13]

'Le Bosch fini'   *'The end of the Bosch.'*

Russians against Germans in East Prussia, Austrians fighting
Serbs near Belgrade, the French on the border with Belgium
defending their country against the Germans – on all these
fronts, in the first weeks of the war, armies advanced and
retreated, towns were captured and relieved. Then the French
Army, battered by German guns, dug in, holding their ground
in deep trenches and underground shelters. The same thing
happened on other fronts, and by the end of 1914, opposing
armies had become almost stationary. In northern France, they
stayed stationary for most of the war. Crouched or stood down
out of sight perhaps only fifty yards from the enemy, two
armies faced each other, fired at and raided each other across
the unoccupied space of no man's land.

Some thought the war was heroic and splendid, a bit like a
game. There were examples of British officers leading men
into action by 'kicking off', booting a football towards the
enemy. Private L S Price remembered such a moment.

As the gunfire died away I saw an infantryman climb onto the para-
pet into no man's land, beckoning others to follow. As he did so he
kicked off a football. A good kick. The ball rose and travelled toward
the German line. That seemed to be the signal to advance.[14]

One fatal mistake for the British was a lack of imagination. The historian John Laffin describes British preparations for the assault that was to begin the Battle of the Somme, in 1916, in which more than a million men died in the space of four months.

Rehearsals for the big assault were farcical. Acres of dusty ground were lined with tapes to represent trenches and the men then assaulted and 'captured' the tapes. Everything was done in the imagination. The soldiers were ordered to imagine gas, barbed wire and artillery fire. Men with flags were posted in front of the advancing waves to represent bursting British shells. The attackers were then told, 'Imagine that you are wearing full gear, and that you are carrying wire, bombs and pigeons.' And all the time there was an insistence on a steady walk. The Staff had convinced themselves that the troops would become confused if other tactics were employed – such as rushing from cover to cover, firing on the move or following close upon a creeping barrage from their own guns. This belief resulted from the idea, prevalent among British regulars, that the volunteers of Kitchener's army were very dull men. This was not so; many intelligent men had responded to the call for the New Army.

The rehearsals were carried out in silence, by numbers, and as a drill. Unrealistic and impractical, they gave the troops no sense of battle, merely the dangerously misleading impression that the initial assault would be a walkover.

With the backing of his senior staff officers, Rawlinson prescribed an assault by four rows of advancing infantry. He was prepared to admit that two or three rows sometimes succeeded in capturing enemy positions, but four rows was a much more certain method. It is not a matter of hindsight to say that, in effect, Rawlinson was planning to bring about heavy casualties among his own men. He was simply giving German machine-gun bullets a better target. His four-row advance was an almost incomparable tactical blunder.

Rawlinson issued instructions that advancing troops were not to charge, merely to walk.[15]

On 1 July 1916, after a seven-day artillery bombardment, the British infantry on the Somme attacked the German Second Army. At the start of the battle a German machine-gunner could hardly believe what he saw.

We were surprised to see them walking, we had never seen that before. The officers went in front. I noticed one of them walking calmly, carrying a walking stick. When we started to fire we just had to load and reload. They went down in their hundreds. We didn't have to aim, we just fired into them.[16]

**During the first day of the battle, the British Army alone suf-
fered 50,000 casualties, the largest number ever lost by the
British in one day. The Germans also suffered badly, although
the Allies did not realize this at the time. British Brigadier
General Rees, General Officer commanding the 94th Infantry
Brigade on 1 July, thought he'd seen 'a marvellous advance'.**

They advanced in line after line, dressed as if on parade, and not a
man shirked going through the extremely heavy barrage, or facing
the machine-gun and rifle fire that finally wiped them out. I saw the
lines which advanced in such admirable order melting away under
the fire. Yet not a man wavered, broke the ranks, or attempted to
come back. I have never seen, I would never have imagined, such a
magnificent display of gallantry, discipline and determination. The
reports I have had from the very few survivors of this marvellous
advance bear out what I saw with my own eyes, viz, that hardly a
man of ours got to the German front line.[17]

Far away, on the Italian border, there were dug-outs high in the mountains, in the snow. Paolo Monelli, an Italian major, describes his.

Snow on snow. Snow from the dun sky, snow from the dun ground, which the wind lifts, snow at the entrances of the burrows in the snow. Our war with winter is beginning – with its dead, with its wounded.

There has been time to make but few huts, and those are groggy owing to the bad weather and insufficient materials: tunnels of snow lead to the warm dens dug out of the rock, caves of darkness and stench, and it's hard work for a candle to penetrate that thick fug: inside them lie the men who come in frozen and dripping from duty.

Then the wind rises, and the blizzard steams all round; the tracks, the path, the mountainside, and the holes disappear from view, and a uniform whitewash is spread over everything. The entrance to our dens is stopped up; the snow piles up in the burrow against canvas that acts as a curtain, and in the doorway, which little by little becomes closed, levelled, annihilated, in the vaporous uniformity. Every trace is blotted out. A man who was lost and wandering on the mountain now would never believe that there are people buried in its inside, living lads who breathe and eat and sleep and play cards by candlelight. If you want to know where the entrance to a dugout is, you must look carefully for the tip of the stick which has been stuck up close by to guide one to it.[18]

Fug   Hot, smoky atmosphere.

Living quarters away from the front line were quite different, and even at the front some British underground shelters in drier, chalkier ground were quite comfortable. The historian John Ellis describes one.

In the Arras sector in early 1916 there was at least one shelter that was thirty feet deep. Made up of two small rooms, one decorated with pink wallpaper and one with green, it also contained a bed, several easy chairs, a stove, a mantelpiece and a large mirror.[19]

John Ellis also gives us a picture of German luxury behind the front line.

But further back the accommodation was, under the circumstances, almost lavish. Such was the case in the Somme Valley in 1916. Here the dug-outs were thirty or forty feet deep, connected by tunnels and steel railway systems. Electric light and ventilation was provided in all rooms, and many of them had panelled walls and planked floors. An English chaplain who visited some captured German trenches during the Battle of the Somme described the extreme lengths to which the Germans went to make these dug-outs habitable. The walls were boarded with neatly morticed timbers, telephone wires were laid along the walls, iron girders were boxed in, ceilings were painted white, woodwork varnished, and in the officers' quarters one even found wooden beading, carpets on the floors and glass windows.[19]

Flora Sandes was an Englishwoman who went out to nurse soldiers in Serbia. Her experience was very unusual, perhaps unique. By degrees, she was drawn into becoming a soldier.

Looking back, I seem to have just naturally drifted by successive stages, from a nurse into a soldier.

The soldiers in the Ambulance seemed to take it for granted that anyone who could ride and shoot, and I could do both, would be a soldier, in such a crisis. To their minds there was nothing particularly strange about a woman joining up, there had occasionally been

Serbian peasant girls in the army, and there was one in this same regiment. The only thing that distinguished me particularly, and made them treat me with so much affection and respect, was the fact that I, an Englishwoman, was willing to rough it with them, and to fight for Serbia. Like the Turks they say, 'to die for your country is not to die'; but to die for someone else's country they thought to be something extra special.

So, when the brigade holding Baboona Pass began slowly to retreat towards Albania, where there were no roads, and we could take no ambulances to carry the sick, I took the Red Cross off my arm and said, very well, I would join the 2nd Infantry Regiment as a private.

When the 'commandant' of the regiment, Colonel Militch, laughingly took the little brass figure '2' off his own epaulettes, and fastened them on the shoulder-straps of his 'new recruit,' as he called me, it seemed a 'fait accompli,' and official sanction came when we reached Bitol before going into Albania. There Colonel Militch took me with him to Colonel Vasitch, the commandant of the division, and he told me that, though I could even then get back to Salonique by the last train leaving that night, it would be better for the Serbs if I joined the army and went through Albania with them, as the simple peasant soldiers already looked upon me as a sort of representative of England, and a pledge, and if I stuck to them it would encourage them, and strengthen their belief that in the end England would help them.[20]

For some, the war meant imprisonment. Aladar Kuncz, a German prisoner, was in the Ile D'Yeu prison in France for four years, trying to stay sane.

When a man has lost everything, and his life hangs by no more than a hair, he watches over it with an aching anxiety that he never had for the riches of his former life. I had nothing left but the empty, beastly inaction of my fourth year in imprisonment – the mattress in the casemate, the daily turnips, the ever-dwindling bread ration – yet I clung to it with a wild, instinctive stubbornness, watched over it restlessly that my consciousness should not slip from it, for if it once left that fragment nothing else could follow but an endless, dark wandering in madness.

· ·

I got up glad only to hear the bugle, glad of the thin coffee and the watery, tasteless vegetables, glad to see the soldiers' bayonets, and if in those heavily passing hours and days I felt consciousness again trying to leave me I ran out into the yard, trod out the counted steps of my walk, shut my eyes, ears, spirit to the vertigo of temptation, and blind and deaf and thoughtless ran and ran till I had left the haunting behind me and nothing was left but the life of a prisoner.

· ·

The number of serious nerve cases increased in that fourth winter. Two Germans went raving mad. They were taken to a French lunatic asylum, and there they died. The other cases were only wrecks, but apparently there was enough life in them to prevent them being sent home.[21]

Horrific though the war was, there were stories of men in other occupations near the front who had urges to be in the fighting themselves. Aubrey Herbert tells one.

We have a clerk there, Venables. He has got tired of writing, and, wanting to change the pen for the sword, borrowed a rifle and walked up to the front line at Quinn's Post. There he popped his head in and said: 'Excuse me, is this a private trench, or may anyone fire out of it?'[22]

In April 1917 the USA joined in the war against Germany, and by July 1918 F W Graser was in the front line. As with many soldiers, the memory of a near miss stayed with him for the rest of his life.

I was on communications between our battery and our Battalion Headquarters which were further back, running lines out in the open. The only dug-out was for the top officers. During that first night our battery telephone was in an old farmhouse, and we had decided that we would put our blankets down in this farmhouse and the ones who ranked topmost put their blankets at the back of the house. Being lower ranking I had mine in a room at the front. It quieted down a little bit in the morning and after running lines all night I came in to rest up a little bit. I went upstairs and looked in my room and there was a hole about eight or ten inches in diameter – one hole in the entire building! – and my blankets where I'd made my bed were shredded. From then on, all my life I've figured, why, I'm living on grace. I never worried from that time on. It gave me the feeling that if it's intended you'll be there, you'll *be* there! They gave us lectures in the USA, and they quoted statistics. A certain percentage would be wounded and have to go home, a certain percentage would be killed. But they led us to expect that the odds were all in favour of getting back home safe and sound. We took some powerful casualties though. We figured their statistics were somewhat optimistic.[23]

Running lines   *Laying telephone lines between batteries.*

Soldiers are not always loyal and disciplined. Charles Yale Harrison describes a breakdown in discipline amongst battle-weary British troops in 1918 in France.

We halt. We are in one of the main streets. On both sides of the street are stores – grocery stores, tobacco shops, clothing stores, wine-shops. In the windows we see displays of food and cigarettes tempt-ingly displayed – tins of lobster, glass jars of caviare, tinsel-capped magnums of champagne. I look through a glass window and read: *Veuve Cliquot* – the bottle looks important and inviting. In another window I read: 'Smoke De Reszke cigarettes.'

We ask our captain – a fidgety, middle-aged man by the name of Penny – why the town is deserted. He explains that the Germans dropped a few long-range shells into the city a few days ago, and the inhabitants, thinking that Heinie was about to enter, fled leaving the city as we now see it.

We rest on the kerb of the street, looking hungrily at the food and cigarettes behind the thin glass partitions. Little knots of soldiers gather and talk among themselves.

As I stand talking to Broadbent a man in the company ahead of us idly kicks a cobble-stone loose from its bed. He picks it up and crashes it through a wide, gleaming shop window. The crash and the sound of the splintering, falling glass stills the hum of conversation. The soldier steps through the window and comes out with a basketful of cigarettes. He tosses packages to his comrades.

Another crash!

More men stream through the gaping windows.

Officers run here and there trying to pacify the men.

As far as I can see, men are hurling stones through windows and clambering in for supplies.

The street is a mass of scurrying soldiers.

Discipline has disappeared.

I step through an open, splintered window and soon come out laden with tins of peas, lobster, caviare, bottles of wine. Broadbent and I visit many shops. In each are crowds of soldiers ransacking shelves, cupboards, cellars. Some of them are chewing food as they pillage.

When we have filled our bags with food, drink and cigarettes, we make off to look for a place to rest.[24]

For both sides in northern France, having to live, be wounded or die so near to the opposing trenches brought a special horror. For one German soldier, Ernst Toller, it became impossible to think of 'German or Frenchman'.

One night we heard a cry, the cry of one in excruciating pain; then all was quiet again. Someone in his death agony, we thought. But an hour later the cry came again. It never ceased the whole night. Nor the following night. Naked and inarticulate the cry persisted. We could not tell whether it came from the throat of German or Frenchman. It existed in its own right, an agonized indictment of heaven and earth. We thrust our fingers into our ears to stop its moan; but it was no good: the cry cut like a drill into our heads, dragging minutes into hours, hours into years. We withered and grew old between those cries.

Later we learned that it was one of our own men hanging on the wire. Nobody could do anything for him; two men had already tried to save him, only to be shot themselves. We prayed desperately for his death. He took so long about it, and if he went on much longer we should go mad. But on the third day his cries were stopped by death.

I saw the dead without really seeing them. As a boy I used to go to the Chamber of Horrors at the annual fair, to look at the wax figures of Emperors and Kings, of heroes and murderers of the day. The dead now had that same unreality, which shocks without arousing pity.

I stood in the trench cutting into the earth with my pick. The point got stuck, and I heaved and pulled it out with a jerk. With it came a slimy, shapeless bundle, and when I bent down to look I saw that wound round my pick were human entrails. A dead man was buried there.

A – dead – man.

What made me pause then? Why did those three words so startle me? They closed upon my brain like a vice; they choked my throat and chilled my heart. Three words, like any other three words.

A dead man – I tried to thrust the words out of my mind; what was there about them that they should so overwhelm me?

A – dead – man –

And suddenly, like light in darkness, the real truth broke in upon me; the simple fact of Man, which I had forgotten, which had lain deep buried and out of sight; the idea of community, of unity.

A dead man.

Not a dead Frenchman.

Not a dead German.

A dead man.

All these corpses had been men; all these corpses had breathed as I breathed; had had a father, a mother, a woman whom they loved, a piece of land which was theirs, faces which expressed their joys and their sufferings, eyes which had known the light of day and the colour of the sky. At that moment of realization I knew that I had been blind because I had wished not to see; it was only then that I realized, at last, that all these dead men, Frenchmen and Germans, were brothers, and I was the brother of them all.[25]

AT SEA
AND IN THE AIR

**There was also a war being waged under the sea. British sub-
marines and German U-boats sank warships and merchant
ships carrying food and materials to each other's ports. One
way of combating U-boats was to disguise armed ships as
unarmed merchant-ships. Such Q-ships, as they were called,
would tempt the U-boat to the surface, so they could attack
with their deck guns, thus saving precious torpedoes. Here
Commander Francis Grenfell describes such an encounter.**

She seemed to come up very slowly at first, and kept turning first in
one direction and then in another, for the purpose, we thought, of
bringing her gun to bear, as it seemed to be abaft the conning tower.
Some of her shots fell pretty close, and all seemed to burst on impact
with the water, giving off a black smoke. Some hands were now
directed to stand at the rail and point her out to each other, and to
move about on deck in view of the submarine. I have a mental picture of Pym and Cox leaning over the rail, watching the sub, and
then coiling up some ropes, as calmly as if in harbour.

After a considerable while the sub seemed to make up its mind,
and come straight for us, firing as she came. I waited until she came
within about 1,000 yards and had just fired another shot, and then
gave the signal to abandon ship. Harrison, the helmsman, and
myself rushed off the bridge, well in view of the sub, Harrison and
the helmsman then finding their way by the lee of the hatches into
the after wheel house above the engines, while I returned on my
hands and knees to the bridge. . . . I crawled like a worm across the
bridge, damning Ashton for adjusting his position and exposing the
top of his head above the rail. . . .

I was now close against the canvas screen running round the
bridge rails, and called to Ashton for a knife to cut a spy-hole
through it. With a dextrous flick he slid the knife along the deck
towards me without exposing an arm. A second later and I had a
small flap cut in the screen, just large enough for one part of my
binoculars. I could now see the submarine steering out to port and
watched her coming round in a big sweep towards us. She did not
fire again after our boats had left. I could see all her people and sung
out a number of particulars of her appearance, which Ashton noted
down.

It was clear now that the sub had no suspicion of our deadly char-
acter, and I was determined that today there should be no doubt
whatever as to the issue – so I waited to let her get as close as she

cared to come. I expected her either to come close alongside or to put some shots into us, or to board and bomb us. Either event would suit us nicely. Instead of stopping on our port side, however, she continued her circle and passed close under the stern, so close that White, in the after gun house, was afraid the people in her would be able to see in through the after gun house ports. I passed the word to the guns that she was coming round to our starboard quarter, and then slithered across the deck and had another spy-hole cut in the screen in a moment. Then I saw her coming round the stern, and when she was on the quarter and the guns were all bearing on her I leapt for the signal bell and signalled 'open fire'.[26]

Helmsman *Person who steers a ship.*
Bridge *Platform from which a ship is commanded.*
After/Abaft *Towards the back.*
Port/Starboard *Left/right-hand side of a ship.*
Stern *The rear of a ship.*

The 1914-18 war was the first in which aeroplanes took part. They were very fragile things, made of wood and canvas and held together by wires. They flew only at about 80 kilometres per hour, and couldn't go far. At the beginning of the war planes were used for reconnaissance and dropping bombs. It hardly occurred to fliers that they could use their planes to attack other planes. British Wing-Commander, W S Douglas carried a rifle 'for safety's sake'.

The first time I ever encountered a German machine in the air, both the pilot (Harvey-Kelly) and myself were completely unarmed. Our machine had not been climbing well, and as I was considered somewhat heavy for an observer, Harvey-Kelly told me to leave behind all unnecessary gear. I therefore left behind my carbine and ammunition. We were taking photographs of the trench system to the north of Neuve Chapelle when I suddenly espied a German two-seater about 100 yards away and just below us. The German observer did not appear to be shooting at us. There was nothing to be done. We waved a hand to the enemy and proceeded with our task. The enemy did likewise. At the time this did not appear to me in any way ridiculous – there is a bond of sympathy between all who fly, even between enemies. But afterwards just for safety's sake I always carried a carbine with me in the air.[27]

When two pilots chased each other round the sky it seemed like an old-fashioned combat between two armed knights. Some fliers became famous, like the German Manfred von Richthofen. He described the end of a fight in the air in the diary he kept. He was shot down and died in 1918.

We were by now deep behind our lines at an altitude of about five hundred metres. I forced the Englishman to make more turns. While turning in an air fight one drops lower and lower until one must land, or attempt to fly straight home. My Englishman decided to do the latter. Lightning-quick the thought came to me: Now the hour for this poor fellow has come! I sat behind him. At the necessary distance, about fifty metres away, I sighted him clearly and pressed my machine-gun buttons. What next! Not a shot came out. A jam in the guns. I cleared them and again pressed the machine-gun buttons: Not a shot! Curses! Success so near! I looked at my machine-guns once more. Blast! I had already shot my last round. I have the empty ammunition belts in my hands. A thousand shots! I had used so many when I did not need them.

Under no circumstances could I allow him to get away, however. To have fought with a red machine for almost a quarter of an hour and to have escaped – that would be a triumph for the English!

I flew closer and closer to him, the distance from my propeller to his rudder constantly decreasing. I estimated: ten metres, five metres, three, now only two metres! Finally a perplexing thought came to me: Shall I strike his rudder with my propeller? Then he would fall, but I should probably go with him. Another thought: If I shut the engine off the minute I touch him, what would happen? Then my Englishman looked round at me, saw me directly behind him, cast a terrified glance at me, shut his engine off, and landed near our third position. Down on the ground he let his engine idle.

When a pilot lands near the enemy, he tries to set fire to his plane to destroy it. In order to prevent this, one shoots in the vicinity of the plane in such cases until the pilot runs away. So I flew over so close to his head that he noticed I was on the alert. The Englishman jumped out of his machine, waved to me and held his hands high, and let himself be taken by our infantry nearby.[28]

Another entry in von Richthofen's diary shows a strange unwarlike attitude to such fighting.

Early in the war I found that when I downed an Englishman, my hunting passion was quenched for the time being. I seldom tried to shoot down two Englishmen, one after the other. If one fell, I had a feeling of absolute satisfaction.[29]

BACK AT HOME

From the beginning of the war, Britain and its allies tried to prevent foodstuffs and other materials from reaching Germany. Lilo Linke, living in Berlin, experienced as a child the effects of the blockade.

Soon after the outbreak of the war the food shortage began. In the end we could hardly buy a pea without a ration card. No fat, no milk, no eggs, and Fritz [my brother] and I needed them so urgently.
. . . .
   Day after day we had to queue up for the barest necessities of life. . . . Thawed snow covering the pavement with wet mud. Drumming rain. Or a biting wind. And freezing cold. Along the houses, in front of every sixth shop, long rows of women and children, four abreast, pressed against each other and the walls. For hours before the shop was opened, the colourless crowd stood waiting, bent down by weather and misery, distortions of mankind. Yet a single policeman was enough to keep hundreds of them in their places.
   Under-nourished and thinly dressed, too tall for my ten years, I stood among them to get a piece of meat or a pound of bones. My numb hand was scarcely able to hold the money and the ration card. Anxiously I thought of my mother. She was as thin as a lost goat and looked old and ugly with her sunken cheeks and the blue rims around her eyes. She never ate her full rations but went without in order to feed Fritz and me a little better than our own tiny share would have allowed her. Now she was queuing up at the grocer's round the corner for ounces of sugar and flour more precious than caviare. Would she get it? Or would the supply be sold out again before it was her turn?[30]

**For families in Britain with men and lads at home, the intro-
duction of conscription – in January 1916 – was a threatening
event. Edith Gaskell's father was a member of the local
tribunal that decided whether men should go to war or stay at
home working.**

Then things began to be serious. Losses were heavy and more men
were going to be needed – so conscription came and all men of eligi-
ble age received their Calling-up Papers – a sad occasion for most
of them. Some, of course, could not be excused, but a few others
were supposed to hold jobs which were as necessary as fighting. But
how to decide who should go and who should stay comfortably at
home, that was the problem. So, tribunals were set up, of senior
gentlemen of the village, to judge each case and decide, after hearing
the reasons, excuses and pleadings, etc., of the young men concerned.

Some of the senior gentlemen seemed to take a pride and pleasure
in their importance – no doubt thinking, also, that they were 'Doing
Their Bit'; but some hated the job and I think my father was one of
these – being sensitively aware that his judgement might mean life
or death to someone.

Secret visits were made to him after dark. A young man, perhaps
accompanied by his wife or girl-friend, would explain how necessary it was that he should remain at home. Father would say, in sympathy, that he would 'Do his best', which meant exactly that and
they would go away with an over-optimistic idea of what he meant,
but, of course, a Tribunal member had, in any case, only one vote.[31]

Some men refused, for reasons of conscience, to go to war. They became known as conscientious objectors. British 'conchies' were often treated badly. Such handling was sometimes so brutal that it amounted to torture.

This is an account of what happened to one conchie, Gray, who wouldn't give in to pressure.

One day his arms were trussed up his back by force, he was tied in that position with a rope, and a man then pulled him round the field by the rope, walking, running, etc., alternately. On another day he was stripped naked, a rope tightly fastened round his abdomen, and he was then pushed forcibly and entirely immersed in a filthy pond in the camp grounds eight or nine times in succession and dragged out each time by the rope. The pond contained sewage. He says the effect of the tightening of the rope after the second immersion cannot be described, and was still more intolerable when, after the last immersion, they put upon his wet and muddy body a sack with a hole through for the head and one for each arm.[32]

After conscription, and with so many men away or injured, women began to do work that had always been reserved for men. This is the historian A J P Taylor's summary of what happened.

Lloyd George went further in his search for more munition workers. Shortly after he became Minister of Munitions, the militant suffragettes staged a final demonstration under their leader, Christabel Pankhurst. They marched down Whitehall with the slogan: 'We demand the right to work.' Lloyd George gave them this right. Many hundred thousand women were brought into the shell factories.

Others became typists in business and government offices: the male office-clerk vanished for ever. For the first time, women were earning their own living on a massive scale. They went into public houses, and paid for their own drinks. The girls in factories and offices needed more sensible clothes. Their skirts became shorter; they were no longer held in by tight corsets. Many of them cut their hair. Women took over as tram conductors. A little later, the armed forces started auxiliary services for women, who wore their own khaki uniform. There were women police. Other belligerent countries followed the same pattern, though none carried it so far as Great Britain. By the end of the war, it was no longer true that woman's place was in the home.[33]

After soldiers had been back at home for a while, on leave or convalescing, partings were hard to bear. Helen Thomas, wife of the English poet Edward Thomas, describes their last moments together. He was killed in action in April 1917.

'And here are my poems. I've copied them all out in this book for you, and the last of all is for you. I wrote it last night, but don't read it now . . . It's still freezing. The ground is like iron, and more snow has fallen. The children will come to the station with me; and now I must be off.'

We were alone in my room. He took me in his arms, holding me tightly to him, his face white, his eyes full of a fear I had never seen before. My arms were around his neck. 'Beloved, I love you,' was all I could say. 'Helen, Helen, Helen,' he said, 'remember that, whatever happens, all is well between us for ever and ever.' And hand in hand we went downstairs and out to the children, who were playing in the snow.

A thick mist hung everywhere, and there was no sound except, far away in the valley, a train shunting. I stood at the gate watching him go; he turned back to wave until the mist and the hill hid him. I heard his old call coming up to me: 'Coo-ee!' he called. 'Coo-ee!' I answered, keeping my voice strong to call again. Again through the muffled air came his 'Coo-ee'. And again went my answer like an echo. 'Coo-ee' came fainter next time with the hill between us, but my 'Coo-ee' went out of my lungs strong to pierce to him as he strode away from me. 'Coo-ee!' So faint now, it might be only my own call flung back from the thick air and muffling snow. I put my

hands up to my mouth to make a trumpet, but no sound came. Panic seized me, and I ran through the mist and the snow to the top of the hill, and stood there a moment dumbly, with straining eyes and ears. There was nothing but the mist and the snow and the silence of death.

Then with leaden feet which stumbled in a sudden darkness that overwhelmed me I groped my way back to the empty house.[34]

LOOKING AFTER THE WOUNDED AND DYING

About eight and a half million soldiers died in the First World War. It is hard to imagine death on such an enormous scale. But it would have been even worse without the nurses, doctors, stretcher-bearers, ambulance-drivers, and hospital orderlies who worked near the fighting.

Two Russian nurses, Sophie Botcharsky and Florinda Pier, saw a German gas attack catch up with some Russian soldiers. The horrible effects of gas included blindness, deafness, fever and difficult breathing.

The firing stopped suddenly, and the silence startled us. There was a feeling that in this quiet something dreadful must be brewing, and we went out of the house to gaze down the road. Off towards the trenches a group of men came running with desperate speed. As they drew near we saw that their faces were yellow, and some were sick as they ran. At first we thought they were coming to us, but when we realized that they were going to run blindly by us, we shouted to know what had happened; without turning their heads, almost without seeing us, they tore past and on down the road. Then we heard the galloping of a horse and our own ambulance, which was always on duty by the communication trenches, approached, rocking with its speed. The two student orderlies, hatless and wide-mouthed with horror, drove past, crying that everyone had been wiped out; and as they went by we saw that the ambulance was empty. It was inexplicable; what, in perfect silence, could create uncontrollable panic? Out of the forest men broke, and running across a field disappeared into a second forest and were lost to view. We stood baffled and oppressed.

Finally one man paused for breath, and gasping out, 'We are being poisoned like rats, the Germans are sending a fog that is following us –' he went on down the road.

Schnackenbourg for once lost his nonchalance, and ordered us all to go to the second wood in which the men had taken shelter. A small boy who had attached himself to our Unit refused to leave, and standing in the doorway with a pot of jam in the pocket of his jacket, from which he kept scooping out the sweet stuff with his finger, caught up a rifle and shouted, 'They can walk over my dead body, but I will fight to the last drop of my blood.'

We left him to do it and tore down the road; once in the shelter of the trees we waited. Schnackenbourg found one of our orderlies who had been in the communication trenches, and with staring eyes the

man said that when the firing had stopped he had gone forward to look at a yellow fog which lay on the ground some distance ahead. Then men had rushed from the trenches with blue faces, froth on their lips, and just before reaching him had fallen dead. He still seemed to see the dreadful sight. It was the men who had seen this who had turned and fled. Still we waited in the wood, not knowing what to do; more men gathered about us, silent and gloomy, some sick, all in the grip of panic.[35]

Doctors and nurses, however well-trained, were unprepared for the effects of mass war. Sister Helen Dora Boyston, a US nurse, found it hard to cope with the sheer number of wounded coming in.

Our first warning that the convoys were coming was the steady hum of ambulances winding down the road as far as the eye could see, with scarcely a yard between them. Nearly every case should have been a stretcher case. Ragged and dirty; tin hats still on; wounds patched together any way; some not even covered.

They were direct from the line and their faces were white and drawn and their eyes glassy from lack of sleep. There were great husky men, crying with the pain of gaping wounds and dreadfully discoloured trench feet. There were strings of from eight to twenty blind boys filing up the road, their hands on each other's shoulders and their leader some bedraggled, bandaged, limping youngster.

Matron sent us to the D Lines. She said that there were 500 in this convoy, and that there were stretcher cases on the way, and she asked if my friend Ruth, myself and Topsy Stone could clean up the 500 walkers. We thought that we could, though heaven knows how we thought we were going to do it. We made a frantic effort to systematize our work. We made a small table for the medical officer, and then a large table piled with bandages, splints, boric ointment, sponges and a basinful of Dakins for wet dressings. Then there were two smoky lanterns and an enfeebled primus stove.

Ruth, armed with a pair of scissors, stood in the doorway and beckoned the boys in, two or three at a time. Because there was so much to do it was impossible to try to take the stiff, dried bandages off carefully. The only thing to do was to snatch them off with one desperate tug. Poor Ruth! She could hardly stand it. She'd cut the dressing down the middle, the poor lad looking on with set jaw and imploring eyes. Ruth's own eyes were full. There'd be a quick jerk; a sharp scream from the lad; a sob from Ruth; and he was passed on to the Medical Officer, and Ruth began on the next.

The Medical Officer looked at the wound, said 'Wet – dry – boric ointment' or 'Splint' to the orderly sitting at the table. The orderly scribbled the order on a bit of paper and gave it to the lad, who moved on to Topsy and me. They came much too fast for us, and within fifteen minutes were standing twenty deep around the dressing-table. As the hours went by we ceased to think. We worked through the night until dawn.[36]

The USA declared war on Germany in 1917, but Americans joined the war – if not the fighting – from the beginning. No American citizen could legally enlist as a soldier in a foreign army, so they did other things to help. By 3 September 1914, Red Cross volunteers were gathering in New York. One Red Cross volunteer, Graham Carey, had just left Harvard at the age of twenty-two. He arrived in Paris on 14 December 1914.

I went to France with the idea of being a hospital orderly, but when I got to the American hospital in Neuilly in Paris I found they were organizing ambulances, so I immediately signed up. I already knew how to drive because my father had one of the first private cars. Of course, in those days you had to have a chauffeur, not only to drive it but to attend to it and be responsible for it, and there were great difficulties in driving those early cars. Unbeknown to my father I went out on various occasions with the chauffeur and took over the wheel and got some knowledge of how to drive. I don't know about the other boys. Some of them probably had never driven at all and I certainly wasn't very good, but somehow we managed and soon I was an old hand.[37]

Carolyn Clark, an American nurse, describes her pleasure at being appreciated by the wounded.

The boys came in ambulances and had a hard ride. When they were lifted out they would smile at us, with their eyes only if they were very weak. Occasionally one would say: 'Gee, what a ride,' but usually it was 'Hello' or 'What part of the States are you from?' or 'It's six months since I've seen an honest-to-God American girl.'

When we had a rush of patients they would often have to wait a long time, and we would give them cigarettes and chewing gum and try to fix them up comfortably on their stretchers. There was no grumbling over the long waits. Often when it came to a man's turn he would say: 'Take the other feller first, he's hurt worse than me.' In the operating room they would take ether almost as if they liked it, and some really were 'glad of a chance to go to sleep'.[38]

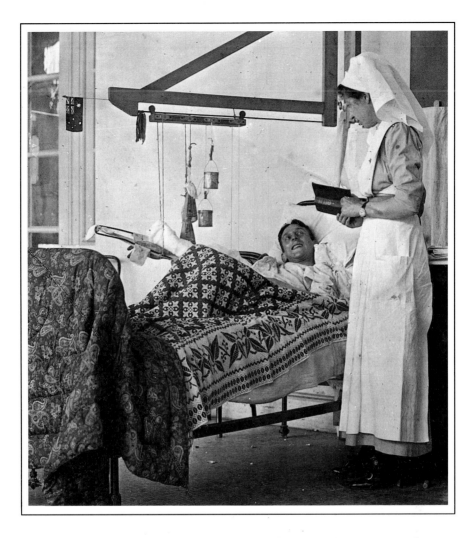

On another front, in Serbia, were many British women volunteers. Flora Scott, who had left her own private nursing home in England, had volunteered to work with soldiers who had typhus. Amid the long months of trying to help the wounded and dying, there were one or two lighter moments.

One poor soul, with gangrene feet and quite unable to move from his bed, handed me a warm new-laid egg each morning. We couldn't imagine where he got it from. One day the doctor came to examine the poor fellow, and when his bed clothes were turned back there lay a hen! His source of new-laid eggs! No one seemed to find it particularly odd or terrible to have eggs laid in bed![39]

ENDINGS

By summer 1918 there were a million fresh American troops in France. On the other side, the German, Austrian, Turkish and Bulgarian armies were exhausted. In September Bulgaria surrendered. Next, Turkey signed an armistice, followed, early in November, by Austria. Then the German Army was driven back, and by 11 November the fighting was over.

Though an armistice had been declared, the guns didn't stop firing before 11 o'clock on 11 November. An American Sergeant, T Grady, made a sad entry in his diary.

11 November – Monday
Cold and raining. Runner in at 10.30 with order to cease firing at 11.00 a.m. Firing continued and we stood by. 306th Machine-Gun Company on my right lost twelve men at 10.55, when a high explosive landed in their position. At 11.00 sharp the shelling ceased on both sides and we don't know what to say. Captain came up and told us that the war was over. We were dumbfounded and finally came to and cheered – and it went down the line like wildfire. I reported Jones' death and marked his grave. Captain conducted a prayer and cried like a baby. Built a big fire and dried our clothes and the bully beef tasted like turkey. We told the new boys our tales and about the battles and they were heavy listeners. Other teams returned from outposts and we celebrated by burning captured ammunition and everything that would burn.[40]

US Army Sergeant Tom Brady describes the excitement of arriving back in New York City.

24 April – Thursday
Passed through the 'Narrows' 7.30. Far Rockaway and Coney Island looked good. Decks were jammed with troops. Small boats carrying girls came out to meet us. Major-General came out to welcome us. . . . There were other boats and tugs loaded with friends. Some carried placards, displaying the name of some boy on board. Passed 'Liberty' and steamed up the river to Pier 54. People working in the big office buildings waved flags and threw out ticker tape. Took three hours to dock. Red Cross nurses lined the pier and a Marine Band played 'There Will Be a Hot Time etc.', 'How Dry I Am' and other old songs, and the boys yelled themselves hoarse. Pulled into the big shed and we received some real lemon pie, coffee and chocolate from the Red Cross. Piled on to a ferry and went down round the Battery and up the North River to the Long Island Railroad. We received a rousing welcome all along. Every steamboat saluted us with their siren horns and bells. The Red Cross put over another barrage of apples, sponge cake and milk. Boarded electric trains and there is some difference betwixt these and the 'Hommes and Chevaux'. A pretty young miss ran out and planted a nice big kiss on a Company 'D' man, only to find out that it was a case of mistaken identity. Another fainted when she met her son. There was a mixture of tears, laughter and whooping and it looked like a 'free for all' as the 'Sweeties' clashed with their heroes. The boys are like a bunch of kids and feel very jubilant. Lieutenant Gorham's wife blew in, and she put an awful barrage of kisses over. I can see now why he shaved off his moustache.

16 May – Friday
Turned in our blankets. Received our discharge and pay 4.00 p.m. Hired a car and beat it to Boston – toot sweet. Just caught the last train home. Finis!!![41]

'Liberty'   *The Statue of Liberty.*
Toot sweet   *Jokey pronunciation of the French phrase* Tout de suite, *meaning 'immediately'.*

The fighting was over, but not the war. As Fred White, a British rifleman, explained, it went on in the minds of those who had taken part.

Us fellows, it took us years to get over it. Years! Long after when you were working, married, had kids, you'd be lying in bed with your wife and you'd see it all before you. Couldn't sleep. Couldn't lie still. Many's and many's the time I've got up and tramped the streets till it came daylight. Walking, walking – anything to get away from your thoughts. And many's the time I've met other fellows that were out there doing exactly the same thing. That went on for years, that did.[42]

The land itself can't seem to forget. More than fifty years after the end of the war, the historian Paul Fussell walked over the killing fields of the Somme, where so many had died.

When the air is damp you can smell rusted iron everywhere, even though you see only wheat and barley. The farmers work the fields without joy. They collect the duds, shell-casings, fuses, and shards of old barbed wire as the plow unearths them and stack them in the corners of their fields. Some of the old barbed wire, both British and German, is used for fencing. Many of the shell craters are still there, though smoothed out and grown over. The mine craters are too deep to be filled and remain much as they were. When the sun is low in the afternoon, on the gradual slopes of the low hills you see the traces of the zig-zag of trenches. Many farmhouses have out in back one of the little British wooden huts that used to house soldiers well behind the lines; they make handy toolsheds. Lurking in every spot of undergrowth just off the beaten track are eloquent little things: rusted buckles, rounds of corroded small-arms ammunition, metal tabs from ammunition boxes, bits of Bully tin, buttons.[43]

Bully tin   *Corned beef tins.*

Important Dates

1914

28 Jun Assassination of Austrian Archduke Franz Ferdinand at Sarajevo.
23 Jul Austrian ultimatum to Serbia.
28 Jul Austria-Hungary declares war on Serbia.
30 Jul Russia orders general mobilization.
1 Aug Germany declares war on Russia. France orders general mobilization.
3 Aug Germany declares war on France.
3/4 Aug Germany invades Belgium.
4 Aug Britain declares war on Germany.
6 Aug Austria-Hungary declares war on Russia.
12 Aug Britain and France declare war on Austria-Hungary.
30 Aug Russian defeat at Battle of Tannenburg, in what is now Poland.
Aug–Sep Battle of the Frontiers. Major German advances.
Aug–Dec Three Austrian attempts to invade Serbia.
6 Sep Battle of the Marne begins, in France. French push back the Germans.
Oct–Nov Battle of Ypres, Belgium.
Nov Turkey enters the war as a German ally.
End of 1914 – Stalemate.

1915

Fighter planes first armed with machine-guns.
Feb German submarine blockade of British Isles begins.
Mar Start of the Dardanelles campaign. British land in Turkey.
Apr–May Second Battle of Ypres. First use of poison gas.
7 May German *U20* sinks the *Lusitania*.
23 May Italy enters the war, on the side of the Allies.
Aug Germany occupies all of Poland.
18 Sep Germany abandons submarine campaign.
Dec–Jan Allies evacuate Gallipoli Peninsula.

1916

25 Jan Conscription for single men introduced in Britain.
Feb–Apr Second German campaign of unrestricted submarine warfare.
Feb–Aug Battle of Verdun, France.
May–Jun Naval battle of Jutland.
Jul–Nov Battle of the Somme, in France; first use of tanks.
Oct Britain begins air attacks on German industrial targets.

1917

Feb Third German campaign of unrestricted submarine warfare.
Mar British Women's Army Auxiliary Corps founded.
British take Baghdad.
6 Apr USA declares war on Germany.
Apr Britain adopts convoy system.
Apr–May Battle of Arras, France.
18 May Conscription introduced in USA.
25 Jun First Americans in France.
Jul–Nov 3rd Battle of Ypres.
Oct Battle of Caporetto, on the Italian border. Italians retreat.
Nov Bolshevik coup in Russia.
Nov–Dec Battle of Cambrai, France.
Dec Russia and Germany sign Armistice at Brest-Litovsk.

1918

Jan US President Woodrow Wilson's 'Fourteen Points', including idea for a League of Nations.
Feb Rationing introduced in parts of Britain.
Mar–Jun Major German offensive on Western Front.
24 Apr German ace fighter pilot, Manfred von Richthofen, shot down and killed.
8 Aug Beginning of Battle of Amiens, France; Germans retreat.
Nov Surrender of German Fleet.
3 Nov Austria-Hungary signs armistice with Allies.
9 Nov German Kaiser abdicates.
11 Nov Armistice between Allies and Germany.

Glossary

Battery   Artillery unit of guns, men and vehicles.
Boric ointment   An antiseptic.
Bosch   French slang for a German soldier.
Carbine   A short firearm, originally used for cavalry use.
Casemate   A chamber in the thickness of the wall, in a fortress.
Cataclysm   A violent event.
Conscription   Compulsory enlistment for military service.
Dakins   Antiseptic solution for treating infected wounds.
Dug-out   Roofed shelter for troops in trenches.
Fug   Fustiness of air.
Gangrene   Death and decomposition of part of the body.
Heinie   American slang for a German soldier.
Kitchener   Lord Kitchener was British Secretary of State for War during the First World War. He was responsible for the voluntary recruitment of three million men – known as Kitchener's Army.
Maxim   A single-barrelled quick-firing machine-gun.
Mobilize   To get forces ready for active service.
Munition workers   People who make ammunition and military weapons.
Reservist   An officer retired from active service, but liable to be called up in an emergency.
Temperance   Abstinence from alcohol.
Trench foot   A disease of the foot caused by standing in water for long periods.
U-boat   German submarine.

Further Reading

A Day that Made History: The first day of the Somme, Richard Tames (Batsford, 1990)
Comrades in Arms: the letters of Frank Cocker, a soldier in the Great War (Tressell Publications, 1988)
Conscientious Objectors, 1916 to the Present Day, Peter Crisp (Tressell Publications, 1988)
Contemporary Accounts of the First World War, J Simkin (Tressell Publications, 1981)
The First World War, edited by Stewart Ross (Wayland, 1989)
Imperial War Museum Book of the First World War, Malcolm Brown (Sidgwick & Jackson, 1991)
Poetry of the First World War, selected by Edward Hudson (Wayland, 1988)
World War I, America at War Series (Facts on File Publications, 1992)

Notes on Sources

1 Quoted in Peter Vansittart, *Voices from the Great War*, p 238 (Cape, 1981).

2 Stephen Graham *Russia and the World* (Cassell, 1915).

3 Ernst Fischer, quoted in Vansittart (op. cit.), p 16.

4 Octavian Taslaunan, *With the Austrian Army in Galicia*, p 10-11 (Skeffington and Sons).

5 Lyn McDonald, *1914-18, Voices and Images of the Great War*, p 10 (Penguin, 1991).

6 Mildred Aldrich, *A Hill Top on the Marne*, p 126 (Constable, 1915).

7 Ernst Toller, *I Was a German*, p 75 (Bodley Head, 1934).

8 Lyn Macdonald, *1914*, p 228 (Michael Joseph, 1987).

9 Isabelle Rimbaud, *In the Whirlpool of War* (Unwin, 1918).

10 Graham (op. cit.), p 77.

11 Ibid. p 88.

12 Macdonald, *Voices* (op. cit.), p 17.

13 William F Pressey, *All for a Shilling a Day*, Imperial War Museum.

14 Quoted in Paul Fussell, *The Great War and Modern Memory*, p 27 (OUP, 1975).

15 John Laffin, *British Butchers and Bunglers of World War One*, p 66 (Sutton, 1988).

16 Ibid., p 68.

17 Ibid., p 66.

18 Paolo Monelli, trans. Orlo Williams, *Toes Up*, p 110 (Duckworth, 1930).

19 John Ellis, *Eye Deep in Hell*, p 18 (John Hopkins, 1976).

20 Flora Sandes, *Autobiography of a Woman Soldier*, p 12 (H F and G Wetherby, 1927).

21 Quoted in Guy Chapman, *Vainglory*, p 631 (Cassell, 1937), from *Black Monastery*.

22 Quoted in Chapman (op. cit.), p 174; from Aubrey Herbert, *Mons, Anzac and Kut*.

23 Macdonald, *Voices* (op. cit.), p 284.

24 Quoted in Chapman (op. cit.), p 636; from Charles Yale Harrison, *Generals Die in Bed*.

25 Toller (op. cit.), p 77.

26 Francis Grenfell, Official Report of Dec 2 1916, quoted in Malcolm Brown, *The Imperial War Museum Book of the First World War*, p 114 (Sidgwick and Jackson, 1991).

27 Quoted in Chapman (op. cit.), p 133.

28 Manfred von Richthofen, *The Red Baron*, p 117, trans. Peter Kilduff (Bailey Bros and Swinfen, 1974).

29 Ibid., p 95.

30 Quoted in Chapman (op. cit.), from *Restless Flags*.

31 Edith Gaskell, unpublished memoir.

32 John W Graham, *Conscription and Conscience*, p 143 (Allen and Unwin, 1922).

33 A J P Taylor, *The First World War*, p 87 (Hamish Hamilton, 1963).

34 Helen Thomas, *Under Storm's Wing* (Carcanet, 1988).

35 Sophie Botcharsky and Florinda Pier, *They Knew How to Die*, p 210 (Peter Davies, 1931).

36 Lyn MacDonald, *The Roses of No Man's Land*, p 284 (Michael Joseph, 1980).

37 Ibid., p 63.

38 Ibid., p 269.

39 Monica Krippner, *The Quality of Mercy*, p 62 (David and Charles, 1980).

40 Macdonald, *Voices* (op. cit.), p 313.

41 Macdonald, *Voices* (op. cit.), p 322.

42 Ibid., p 335.

43 Fussell (op. cit.), p 69.

Index